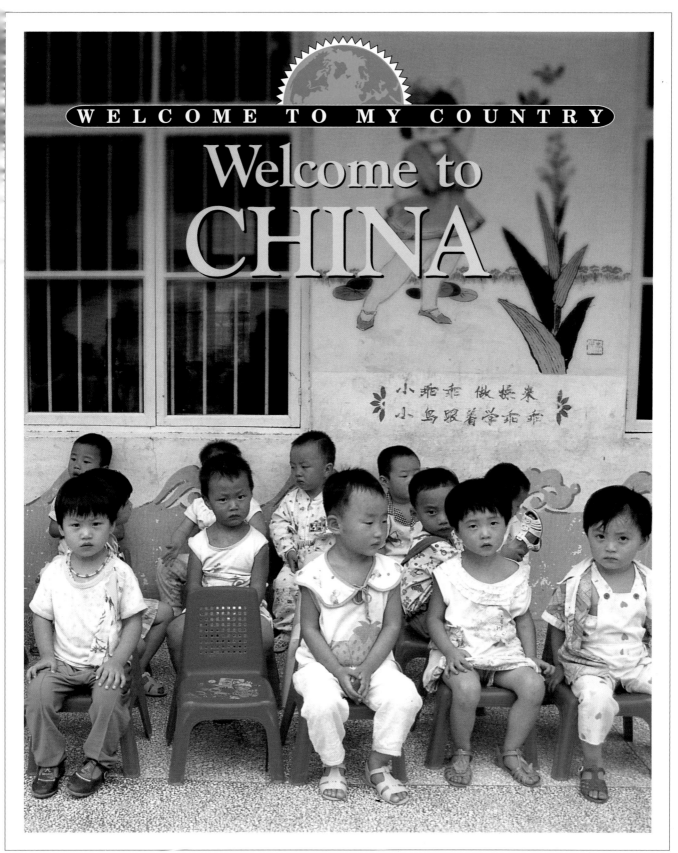

# WELCOME TO MY COUNTRY

# Welcome to
# CHINA

Gareth Stevens Publishing
**MILWAUKEE**

Written by
**Goh Sui Noi/Lim Bee Ling**

Designed by
**Sharifah Fauziah**

Picture research by
**Susan Jane Manuel**

First published in North America in 1999 by
**Gareth Stevens Publishing**
1555 North RiverCenter Drive, Suite 201
Milwaukee, Wisconsin 53212 USA

For a free color catalog describing
Gareth Stevens Publishing's list of high-quality books
and multimedia programs, call
1-800-542-2595 (USA) or
1-800-461-9120 (CANADA)
Gareth Stevens Publishing's
Fax: (414) 225-0377.

© **TIMES EDITIONS PTE LTD 1999**
Originated and designed by
Times Books International
an imprint of Times Editions Pte Ltd
Times Centre, 1 New Industrial Road
Singapore 536196
http://www.timesone.com.sg/te

**Library of Congress Cataloging-in-Publication Data**

Goh, Sui Noi.
Welcome to China / Goh Sui Noi and Lim Bee Ling.
p. cm. — (Welcome to my country)
Includes bibliographical references and index.
Summary: An overview of the history, geography, government,
economy, people, and culture of China.
ISBN 0-8368-2395-8 (lib. bdg.)
1. China—Juvenile literature. [1. China.]
I. Lim, Bee Ling. II. Title. III. Series.
DS706.G645    1999
951—dc21      99-21804

Printed in Malaysia

1 2 3 4 5 6 7 8 9 03 02 01 00 99

**PICTURE CREDITS**
Axiom Photographic Agency: 11
Bes Stock: 4, 5, 7
Camera Press: 15 (bottom), 32 (bottom)
Steve Cohen: 41
Focus Team–Italy: 23
Mark Graham: 6, 26
Dave G. Houser: 38 (bottom), 40
Hutchison Library: cover, 1, 2, 9 (top),
    10 (top), 20, 21, 24, 25, 32 (top), 33
Richard I'Anson: 18
Photobank/Singapore: 34, 38 (top)
Susan Pierres: 29
James C. Simmons: 30 (top)
Topham Picturepoint: 3 (top), 10 (bottom),
    13, 14, 15 (top and center), 27, 30
    (bottom), 36, 45
Trip Photographic Library: 8, 12, 17,
    19, 28, 39
Graham Uden: 3 (bottom), 16, 22, 31,
    35, 37
Yu Hui Ying: 3 (center), 9 (bottom)

Digital Scanning by Superskill Graphics Pte Ltd

# Contents

Words that appear in the glossary are printed in **boldface** type the first time they occur in the text.

# Welcome to China!

More than 1.2 billion people live in China. This means that one in every five people in the world is Chinese! China is an ancient country. Despite its long and troubled past, it enjoys peace and prosperity today. Let's meet the Chinese people and visit their country, the "land of the dragon."

**Opposite:** In China, many people own bicycles — an inexpensive and convenient means of transportation.

**Below:** Located in Beijing, the Forbidden City consists of palaces where China's emperors once lived.

## The Flag of China

The Chinese flag has five yellow stars on a red background. The stars represent the government and the Chinese people. The color red symbolizes **revolution**.

# The Land

Located in East Asia, China is the third largest country in the world following Russia and Canada. It has a land area of 3.7 million square miles (9.6 million square kilometers). Most of the land consists of mountains and **plateaus**. The tallest peak on Earth, Mt. Everest, or Zhumulangma Feng to the Chinese, sits on the border between China and Nepal.

**Below:** Mountains line the border between Qinghai and Gansu provinces.

Plains make up eastern China. **Arid** deserts stretch across western and northern China.

Many people live along China's two longest rivers, the Yangtze, or "Long River," and the Huanghe, or "Yellow River." The Yangtze is the third longest river in the world. The Yellow River is also called "China's Sorrow." It causes great destruction when it overflows its banks during the **monsoon** season.

**Above:** China's Yunnan province boasts beautiful, snowcapped mountains.

## Seasons

China's weather conditions vary greatly because of its size. Northeastern China experiences bitterly cold winters with temperatures as low as 18° Fahrenheit (-8° Celsius). Southern China, however, remains warm all year

round. In the southeastern provinces, the climate is warm and humid. People living on the Qinghai-Tibet Plateau in western China experience cold, but sunny, weather.

**Above:** This lake in Shandong province looks especially beautiful in autumn.

# Plants and Animals

China is home to many kinds of trees, such as oaks, maples, pines, and China cypresses. Flowering plants that grow there include peonies and chrysanthemums. China also provides a home for many unique animals, including the rare golden monkey.

**Below:** Jiuzaigou in northern Sichuan is famous for its spectacular waterfalls.

**Bottom:** The red bear cat, a type of panda, lives in the forests bordering Tibet and India.

The giant panda lives in the mountain areas of central China. Today, pandas face extinction because the bamboo forests that provide their only food source are shrinking.

# History

## Early History

About 500,000 years ago, **primitive** humans lived in caves in China. About 7,000 years ago, the first villages, made of earth and wood, appeared along the Yellow River.

**Above:** During the Shang dynasty, people learned how to make bronze objects. They carved records of their daily lives on some of these objects.

## The First Dynasties

Ancient China was ruled by kings. Each **dynasty**, or line of kings, ruled until another conquered it. The earliest Chinese kingdoms were the Xia, Shang, and Zhou dynasties.

The Zhou king divided his land into territories under the control of dukes and princes. From 770 to 476 B.C., however, many territories fought against each other for land and power. After many years of war, only seven states survived. China's famous **philosopher** and teacher, **Confucius**, lived during this warring period.

**Below:** A boy practices **calligraphy**, the ancient Chinese art of elegant writing.

Two hundred years later, the Qin king defeated all the other states and united China. He called himself *Qin Shihuang* (CHIN shih-huang), or "First Emperor."

The Chinese invented paper and printing. When new land and sea routes were discovered, China began to trade with the rest of the world.

**Left:** Centuries ago, the Silk Road was a trading route connecting China and the West. Today, the Silk Road is still in use, winding through deserts and mountains.

# The Opium Wars

By the early twentieth century, the power of the dynasties had weakened. People were unhappy with the ruling Qing government because it could not protect China from war and foreign occupation. China felt great shame when it lost Hong Kong to Britain in the Opium Wars, a series of battles concerning Britain's sale of **opium** to China.

**Above:** Chiang Kai-shek, a colleague of Sun Yat-sen, helped Sun defeat the warring army generals after the Republic of China was established. After Sun's death in 1925, Chiang became the leader of the Kuomintang.

# Political Struggle

When the Qing dynasty fell in 1911, the Nationalist Party of China, or the Kuomintang, established the **Republic** of China. Dr. Sun Yat-sen, a Western-educated medical doctor, became China's first president.

However, Sun could not bring peace to the new nation. Army generals fought among themselves for power. China also suffered losses when Japan attacked the city of Nanjing in 1937.

**Opponents** of the Kuomintang formed the Chinese Communist Party in 1921. After World War II, the **communists**, led by Mao Zedong, defeated the Kuomintang in 1949 and founded the People's Republic of China. Mao's programs resulted in

**Below:** On October 1, 1949, China and the rest of the world listened as Mao Zedong announced the founding of the People's Republic of China.

disaster and suffering. After Mao died in 1976, Deng Xiaoping became the leader of the Communist Party. Deng introduced many economic changes to **modernize** China.

## Qin Shihuang and the Great Wall

China's first emperor, Qin Shihuang, wanted to protect his country from invaders from the north. In 214 B.C., the walls dividing one territory from another were connected to make one long wall, the Great Wall of China.

## Empress Wu Zetian (625–704)

China's only woman ruler was Empress Wu Zetian. At first, she ruled through her son, the emperor, but in 690, she took the throne herself. China prospered under her leadership.

**Below: The Great Wall of China runs for thousands of miles across China's vast landscape. It is the only man-made object on Earth that is visible from the moon!**

## Sun Yat-sen (1866–1925)

Sun became the Republic's first president when the Qing dynasty collapsed in 1911. He is regarded as the "Father of Modern China."

Dr. Sun Yat-sen

## Mao Zedong (1893–1976)

Mao became the leader of the People's Republic of China in 1949. He rebuilt China by constructing factories, railways, and roads. However, his other programs greatly damaged the economy.

Mao Zedong

## Deng Xiaoping (1904–1997)

Deng, a member of the Communist Party, tried to solve China's economic problems in the 1960s. Government officials reduced Deng's power because he disagreed with some of their policies. After Mao died in 1976, Deng regained power. His programs improved the lives of the Chinese.

Deng Xiaoping

# Government and the Economy

## The Communist Party of China

China is governed by the Communist Party of China. The president, Jiang Zemin, is the head of state.

The National People's Congress elects the president and vice-president. Every five years, the Chinese people choose members of the Congress from throughout China.

**Above:** A farmer tends his flock of geese in Fujian province. Each province is made up of cities and towns that have their own local governments.

# The State Council

China consists of thirty-one provinces, autonomous regions, and **municipalities**. Each of them has a government that reports to the State Council. The State Council is a governmental agency headed by the

prime minister. Its responsibilities include building schools and training doctors and nurses. China's armed forces, police, and courts **enforce** law and order.

**Above:** These children attend school in Sichuan province. The State Council is in charge of health and education.

# Economy

China consists mainly of deserts and mountains. Only one-tenth of the land is suitable for growing crops. Nevertheless, more than 70 percent of China's population farm. In the drier, northern part of the country, farmers grow crops, such as wheat and corn, that can survive without much water. In the warmer, wetter regions of the south, rice is the main crop.

**Below:** People trade wool and other products at a market in one of China's minority regions.

Most of China's electricity is produced from coal. China also mines iron, oil, and tin. These resources allow China to manufacture its own airplanes, ships, cars, and various other machines.

**Above:** The Three Gorges Dam is being built on the Yangtze River.

To gain an additional source of electricity and control floods during monsoon seasons, China is building the world's largest dam, the Three Gorges Dam. Modern railways and roads transport people and goods between major cities.

# People and Lifestyle

Han Chinese are the largest of the fifty-six ethnic groups in China. They make up about 94 percent of the total population. They live mainly along the Yellow and Yangtze rivers and in the northeastern regions. Government policy requires that Han couples in cities must not have more than one child. This is to avoid problems of overcrowding and lack of food.

**Below:** The government introduced the one-child policy in the 1980s. Today, most urban couples have only one child.

## Ethnic Minorities

Most of China's minorities live close to the country's borders. They have their own customs, languages, and beliefs. Kazakhs and Mongolians live in the northern grasslands. They move with their cattle in search of pasture. Most Mongolians are Buddhists, while the Kazahks are Muslims. The Tibetans in southwestern China are farmers or cattle herders. Other ethnic minorities include the Dai, Hui, Li, Uighurs, and Zhuangs.

**Above: Kazakh families live in round tents called yurts.**

# Family Life

For centuries, the teachings of Confucius have influenced the Chinese. They believe that a strong family is the basis of a good society. Everyone is expected to respect and obey their elders. Some Chinese favor sons over daughters because sons carry on the family name and are expected to look after the parents in old age. Confucius also placed great emphasis on education and the arts.

**Below:** In a traditional Chinese family, the elderly live with a son and help take care of their grandchildren.

## Getting Married

In the past, parents chose marriage partners for their children. Today, many young people are free to choose their own partners. In a traditional wedding ceremony, the bride and groom kneel before their elders and offer them tea to show their respect. Then, the couple join family and friends in a lunch or dinner celebration.

**Above:** Women in the countryside often sell handmade crafts, clothing, and embroidery to earn additional income for their families.

# Education

From the age of six, children attend classes between 8 a.m. and 5 p.m. six days a week. Chinese students study many subjects, including history, geography, literature, mathematics, music, and science.

In the countryside and in poor areas, there are few schools. A child may have to walk up to three hours to get to school in these areas.

**Below:** Lunch is served to a group of preschool children.

**Left:** Students in China are skilled on the computer.

After completing six years of primary education, students can go on to attend six years of high school. If they wish to study at a university, they must first pass a national exam.

Since the People's Republic of China was founded, the Chinese Communist Party has made education available to everyone. Adult education was introduced to teach older people who may have missed out when they were young. Today, more than 75 percent of China's adult population can read and write.

# Taoism and Buddhism

The most popular religions in China are Taoism and Buddhism. Taoism is an ancient set of beliefs that teaches people to live in harmony with nature. Chinese Buddhism combines Taoism with other Chinese beliefs and with Indian Buddhism.

**Left:** A monk makes his offerings at a Taoist temple in Xiamen.

Many Chinese believe in gods and nature spirits. They also believe that when a person dies, he or she goes to another world. Family members burn special paper houses, paper cars, and money for the dead. They also place food at the graves.

## Islam and Christianity

Ethnic minorities such as the Kazakhs and Huis are Muslims. Small groups of Christians live in cities such as Beijing and Shanghai.

# Language

The Han Chinese speak many **dialects**, but everyone learns a language called Mandarin. It is also known as *putonghua* (PU-TONG-hua), or "the common language."

All Chinese dialects share one written form. There is no alphabet. Words consist of characters that look like drawings.

**Below:** Streetside comic libraries attract many readers.

## Literature

The earliest Chinese poems date back to about 600 B.C. Many **classical** poems by great poets such as Li Sao are still read and enjoyed today. Drama developed during the Yuan dynasty (1206–1368). The first Chinese novels appeared during the Ming dynasty (1368–1644). Chinese legends and folktales have been handed down for centuries.

**Above:** Mandarin characters are displayed on a barber's wall.

# Arts

Some of China's traditional art forms are thousands of years old. Calligraphy and brush painting survived difficult periods in China's history, when the arts were strictly controlled. Today, many Chinese painters blend traditional brush painting with Western styles. They paint human figures, landscapes, flowers, and animals on silk or paper.

**Above:** These combs are handpainted.

**Below:** Many Chinese paintings feature graceful, yet powerful, animals, such as tigers.

**Left:** An opera actor performs in a colorful warrior costume.

# Chinese Opera

Still popular today, Chinese opera began about nine hundred years ago. The actors wear bright costumes and paint their faces so audiences can recognize their characters easily.

## Music

On important occasions, such as weddings and funerals, Chinese musicians perform with traditional instruments, such as the flute, **zither**, and drums.

**Top:** A traditional music group performs in Yunnan.

## Film

The first Chinese movies were made in the 1920s. Many Chinese actors and directors, such as Zhang Yimou, win international awards today.

**Above:** Gong Li is one of China's most popular actors.

# Folk Crafts

Chinese women practice folk crafts, such as **embroidery** and paper-cutting. During festive seasons, homes are decorated with paper designs. Red is a very popular color during Chinese New Year. The Chinese believe it symbolizes good luck.

**Left:** Many Chinese girls learn the colorful art of embroidery at a young age.

# Leisure

In the past, many Chinese were too poor to enjoy much free time. Today, however, they look forward to a variety of leisure activities. People in cities watch television, go to the movies, and eat at restaurants. In the countryside, people who cannot afford television sets play traditional card games. Some children invent their own games.

**Below:** In the evenings, many couples enjoy ballroom dancing on the sidewalks and in open spaces.

While dance clubs and bowling alleys attract many young people, the older generation still prefers to gather in parks for ballroom dancing, card games, chess, or to chat with friends. Bird owners also bring their songbirds to the parks to compare their singing skills with other birds.

When they are not studying, children enjoy favorite games such as jump rope and hide-and-seek.

**Above:** Card games are a favorite pastime among the older generation.

# Sports

As early as five in the morning, people begin to assemble in the parks for morning exercises.

Traditional exercises, such as *taijiquan* (TAI-chi-CHUAN), or shadowboxing, involve deep breathing to strengthen the body. *Wushu* (WU-shu), or *gongfu* (GONG-foo), involves hand **combat** or fighting with weapons.

**Below:** Many Chinese perform taijiquan outdoors early in the morning.

Popular sports include basketball, table tennis, swimming, and badminton. To promote sports, the government provides sports facilities in factories, schools, and government buildings.

China has achieved outstanding results in many international sports competitions, including the Olympic Games. Its national team excels in gymnastics, track and field, badminton, swimming, and diving.

**Above:** These young people enjoy playing table tennis at a sports stadium in Sichuan.

## Festivals

Chinese people throughout the world celebrate Chinese New Year. Weeks before the festival, every household cleans the house and decorates it with red paper-cuttings. On Chinese New Year's Eve, family members get together for a **reunion** dinner. Children love the festival because they receive *hongbao* (HOHNG-pao), or red packets containing money!

**Top:** New Year celebrations include traditional performances by **stilt-walkers**.

**Above:** These tangerine trees were decorated for the New Year.

## Tomb-Sweeping Day

On April 5, families visit the burial grounds of their ancestors. They sweep the tombs clean to show respect for the dead.

## Dragon Boat Festival

On this day, the Chinese race in dragon boats and eat rice dumplings in memory of Qu Yuan, a poet. Qu Yuan drowned himself when his state was conquered by enemies.

## Mid-Autumn Festival

During this festival, the Chinese gather to admire the full harvest moon and eat **mooncakes**. At night, children carry candle-lit lanterns.

## Minority Festivals

Ethnic minorities have their own festivals. The Dai people in Yunnan province splash water on each other in the spring during the New Year festival to wash away bad luck.

**Above:** The Dai people in Yunnan province drench each other with waterguns during a New Year festival.

# Food

The Chinese people celebrate special occasions with all kinds of delicious food, from dumplings to suckling pig.

A typical Chinese meal, however, is simple. It consists of vegetables, rice, soup, and meat. The Chinese also love to drink tea. In fact, tea drinking began in China about 5,000 years ago.

**Below:** Many kinds of food are available in China. Meals are so important to the Chinese that they greet each other by asking, "Have you eaten?"

Western China, especially the Sichuan province, is known for its spicy food cooked with plenty of chilies. In the eastern regions, people enjoy fresh seafood, such as shellfish and fish, eaten with rice. Northerners in and around Beijing use a lot of chilies and garlic in their food. In the southern part of the country, food is lightly seasoned to bring out its full flavor. China's minority groups have their own unique dishes.

**Above:** Children of all ages like to visit the snack stalls lining the streets of China.

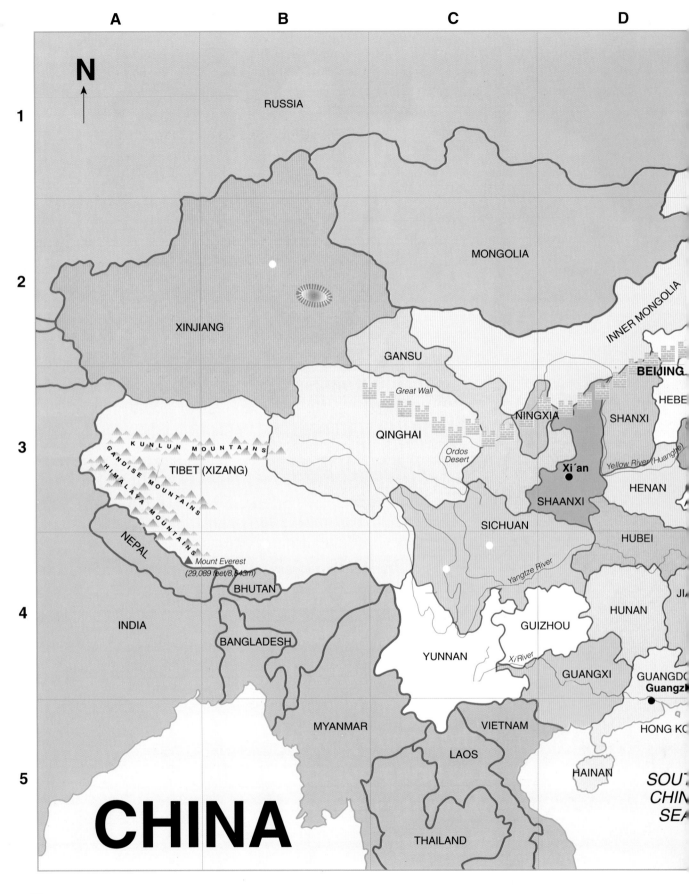

CHINA

| | |
|---|---|
| **Anhui D3** | **Liaoning E2** |
| **Bangladesh B4** | **Mongolia C2** |
| **Beijing D3** | **Myanmar B5** |
| **Bhutan B4** | |
| | **Nanjing E3** |
| **East China Sea E3** | **Nepal A4** |
| **Everest, Mt. A4** | **Ningxia C3** |
| | **North Korea E2** |
| **Fujian E4** | |
| | **Qinghai C3** |
| **Gansu C2** | |
| **Great Wall C3** | **Russia B1** |
| **Guangdong D4** | |
| **Guangxi D4** | **Sea of Japan F2** |
| **Guangzhou D4** | **Shaanxi D3** |
| **Guizhou C4** | **Shandong E3** |
| | **Shanghai E4** |
| **Hainan D5** | **Shanxi D3** |
| **Hebei D3** | **Sichuan C3** |
| **Heilongjiang E2** | **South China Sea D5** |
| **Henan D3** | **South Korea E3** |
| **Himalaya Mountains A3** | |
| | **Taiwan E4** |
| **Hong Kong D5** | **Thailand C5** |
| **Hubei D4** | **Tibet (Xizang) B3** |
| **Hunan D4** | |
| | **Vietnam C5** |
| **India A4** | |
| **Inner Mongolia D2** | **Xi River C4** |
| | **Xiamen E4** |
| **Japan F3** | **Xi'an D3** |
| **Jiangsu E3** | **Xinjiang A2** |
| **Jiangxi D4** | |
| **Jilin E2** | **Yangtze River C4** |
| | **Yellow River (Huanghe) D3** |
| **Kunlun Mountains A3** | **Yunnan C4** |
| | |
| **Laos C5** | **Zhejiang E4** |

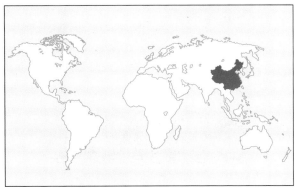

# Quick Facts

**Official Name**     People's Republic of China

**Capital**     Beijing

**Official Language**     Putonghua (Mandarin)

**Population**     1.2 billion

**Land Area**     3.7 million square miles/9.6 million sq. km

**Provinces**     Anhui, Fujian, Gansu, Guangdong, Guizhou, Hainan, Hebei, Heilongjiang, Henan, Hubei, Hunan, Jiangsu, Jiangxi, Jilin, Liaoning, Qinghai, Shaanxi, Shandong, Shanxi, Sichuan, Yunnan, Zhejiang

**Highest Point**     Zhumulangma Feng (Mt. Everest)
(29,089 feet/8,866 m)

**Major Rivers**     Xi River
Yangtze River
Yellow River

**Major Religions**     Buddhism, Islam, Taoism

**Important Festivals**     Chinese New Year (Spring Festival)
Dragon Boat Festival
Mid-Autumn Festival
Tomb-Sweeping Day

**Currency**     Renminbi (RMB 8.3 = U.S. $1 in 1999)

**Opposite:** Beautiful flame trees line the banks of a river in China.

# Glossary

**arid:** very dry.

**calligraphy:** the art of elegant writing.

**classical:** describing a style of literature or art that follows certain ancient rules and forms.

**combat:** fighting.

**communists:** people who support a political system in which the entire community or the government owns all property.

**Confucius:** a Chinese philosopher who believed in the importance of respecting one's elders and in maintaining peace and order in society. Confucius wrote many books about his beliefs.

**dialects:** varieties of a language.

**dynasty:** a line of rulers belonging to the same family.

**embroidery:** the art of decorating a piece of cloth with needlework.

**enforce:** to make sure a rule is obeyed or a belief practiced.

*hongbao* (HOHNG-pao)**:** red packets containing money. Hongbao are given out during the Chinese New Year.

**modernize:** to make new.

**monsoon:** a season of heavy rain.

**mooncakes:** small, round cakes filled with a sweet paste and eaten during the Mid-Autumn Festival.

**municipalities:** big city areas that have some power to govern themselves.

**opium:** the dried juice of the poppy seed, often used as a drug.

**opponents:** enemies; people who disagree with a set of beliefs.

**philosopher:** a person who seeks knowledge about human behavior and the meaning of life.

**plateaus:** large, flat areas surrounded by lower land.

**primitive:** early.

*putonghua* (PU-TONG-hua)**:** the common language; Mandarin.

**republic:** a country where political power rests with the people.

**reunion:** a gathering of relatives or friends after some time apart.

**revolution:** a war in which the people overthrow their leader; a sudden, far-reaching change.

**stilt-walkers:** people who walk and perform on long sticks.

**zither:** a musical instrument with strings stretched over a board.

# More Books to Read

*Ancient China. Eyewitness Books* series. Arthur Cotterell (Knopf)

*Beijing. Cities of the World* series. Deborah Kent (Childrens Press)

*The Children of China: An Artist's Journey.* Song Nan Zhang (Tundra Books)

*The Ch'i-Lin Purse: A Collection of Ancient Chinese Stories.* Linda Fang (Farrar Straus & Giroux)

*China. Festivals of the World* series. Colin Cheong (Gareth Stevens)

*China. Games People Play* series. Kim Dramer (Childrens Press)

*The Great Wall: The Wonders of the World Book.* Elizabeth Mann (Mikaya Press)

*Science in Ancient China. First Book* series. George W. Beshore (Franklin Watts)

*Sichuan Panda Forests. Wonders of the World* series. Terri Willis (Raintree/Steck Vaughn)

*Child Bride.* Ching Yeung Russell (Boyds Mills Press)

# Videos

*China. Windows to the World* series. (Ivn Entertainment)

*Emerging Powers: China.* (New Video Group)

*Great Wall of China. Modern Marvels* series. (A&E Entertainment)

*Mulan.* (Disney Studios)

# Web Sites

www.chinapage.com/

www.solutions.ibm.com/talkingwalls/
   greatwall/gwmain.htm

www.cs.bham.ac.uk/~yxh/tourism.html

www.globalfriends.com/html/
   world_tour/china/china.htm

Due to the dynamic nature of the Internet, some web sites stay current longer than others. To find additional web sites, use a reliable search engine with one or more of the following keywords to help you locate information on China. Keywords: *Beijing, China, Great Wall, Mao Zedong, Ming dynasty, panda, Yellow River.*

# Index